How to Get Free Website Traffic

Contents

Page 2

Use Google Keyword Tool to Increase Your Free Traffic

You want to bring more traffic to your site and you want to do it with no associated costs. Great news! There are several tools you can put to work for you and one of those is the Google Keyword Tool. If you are not familiar with this tool, now is a good time to do so.

The Google Keyword tool can help you find long tail keywords that aren't as competitive and then help you to build content around these words. The most competitive keywords are a real fight to place with and yet most searchers will use alternative keyword searches and those are what you can target with Google Keyword Tools. Not only will you have an increase in traffic you'll have traffic that you would not normally get but that is certainly a fit for your niche.

The Google Keyword Tool Box site is one way to utilize a number of tools that can be of benefit to you and your site. This site contains a number of tools such as Webmaster Central Tool Set, Website Analytics, AdSense Webmaster Income, Free Webmaster Blog, and more. When you take advantage of these tools you can really make the most out of your keywords.

Page 4

If your niche is especially competitive, this is a great way for you to start to build up small recurring traffic so that you can engage the users.

If you want to increase your traffic, you need to be able to bring new visitors to your site. If you continue to use only the keywords or keyword phrases that you always use, then you will only see a slower smaller growth of your traffic.

However, if you choose to look at other related keyboards and expand on your keywords or keyword phrases then you have the opportunity to see your free traffic consistently grow and expand.

Increase Your Site Traffic With Ethical Link Building

Are you looking to increase your site traffic? Would you like to do it for free? If you answered yes, you aren't alone. That's what most of us are trying to do. The key is to increase your traffic ethically, and you can do this with ethical link building.

Link building is very important for your site. This is the process where you create links that point to your page from someone else's page. This happens naturally as quality content is created, but there are also things you can do to build links.

#1 You can trade links with other sites that are directly related to your website's subject matter to bring more traffic to your site. For example, let's say you sell oranges on your site, then you could look to link with other sites that sell oranges or related products like orange juice, orange salad, etc.

You can build two way links that include the other site providing you with a link while you provide them with a link. You should never link to sites that are inferior or low quality as this will threaten your own ranking in the search engines.

You can link back on forums and blogs that are related to your site. Find communities that are in your niche market, create a user profile, enter your site information and then start to make quality posts. This will bring you free traffic to your site.

Page 6

You should also directly contact other sites that are related to your niche. If you can get these companies to link to your website through a blog post or how to article it will significantly increase your free traffic to your site.

Finally, take the time to create an RSS feed, which will allow your articles to easily link to a number of different places. Submit the RSS feed to numerous related directories and give your traffic a direct boost.

Linking is a powerful tool that when used ethically can increase your traffic and your placement in the search engines.

Increase Your Free Traffic with Optimized Articles

If you want to increase your free traffic take advantage of optimized articles. There are three key ingredients to a successful web page/article being optimized:

1. Your meta title

2. Your description 3. Your keywords

This is very simple to fill out and follow when you publish content on your site so take the time to do so. It will help you to begin to rank better and faster with your keywords.

Are you still unsure of what's needed from you? Read on.

A page title is one of the key factors for page ranking and should be given the care and attention it deserves. Your page title tags show up in SERPs or Search Engine Result Pages. Google and other search engines use the title tag as their search results title for that page.

Every page on your site should have its own unique title tag. It should start with a relevant keyword whenever possible. Don't put your company name in the title tag/ The keywords in your title should be in your page and vice versa.

Page 8

Let's look at an example. If your keyword is 'blue jeans' your title could be "Blue jeans at discounted prices" and your first paragraph of your content could start with something like, "Blue jeans are comfortable and rugged and now you can buy them at discounted prices."

Try to avoid stop words, which are words that break up your keywords. For example, blue discount jeans. Discount would be a stop word.

In your meta description you need to provide a short and concise summary of what your site content is. Search engines often display the meta description with your title in the search result pages. Your keyword should also be included here.

You'll have one or more keywords, but you should have one primary keyword and the rest will be secondary. You will use the primary keyword in your title and description.

There it is – optimized articles or content can help to increase free traffic to your site.

Increase Your Free Traffic Using Your Blog

If you are looking for a way to increase your free traffic to your site, consider using your blog. Your blog could be a powerful tool that you are under utilizing.

SEO remains king when it comes to organic search traffic. Your niche will have some popular search terms within it. The more of those you include in your blog the more organic the leads to your blog will be. However, if you include too much text on the main page of your blog, it can be more harmful than good.

Page 10

Use your blog to write about your niche. It doesn't matter what the niche is, make sure to find out what keywords and keyword phrases are trending in that industry or niche, and then make sure that they are included in your blog posts.

You will want to make sure that your blog has a link back to your website that is highly visible. The blog is going to help to increase the visibility of your website and the amount of traffic that your website gets.

Blogs are a form of social marketing. They are often far less formal than your site and share information about your niche whether that is the postings of an expert, opinions about a product/service, information about products or just about anything else that is relevant to your niche. It allows visitors to leave comments and to share your blog posts through other social media channels.

That means you need to give your blog the correct attention. Everything you post should be of quality and it should engage the reader. Doing so means your visitors will return and they will want to share your blog with others that they know. In turn, the number of people that jump from your blog to your website should also increase.

Your blog is an excellent gateway for you to enjoy an increase in traffic on your site, so why not put it to work today?

Page 12

Increase Your Free Traffic Using SEO

If you want to increase free traffic to your website, you need to take advantage of SEO – it's no game, SEO is serious stuff when it comes to doing it right and ensuring you enjoy the benefits of increased traffic flow.

You need to create content that your readers want to read – content that has value. In that content you need to make sure that it is search engine optimized. We don't mean stuffing keywords, but making sure your keywords are used in a natural flow at a rate of about 2% in your content.

Any links you place in your content should be from trusted sites. Even as a new website, there are natural links you can still obtain that are legitimate and recognized by Google and other search engines as acceptable. Don't make the mistake of choosing links that are questionable just so that you have links in your content. You are better off to not have links than you are to have poor links.

Page 14

When you add images make sure that you fill in the image attributes. Pictures do more than dress up the page. The details like caption, title, description and alternate text are important to the search engine. Don't keyword cram but to make sure your keyword(s) are included in your image attributes. Remember some people will search using Google image search rather than text search and if your image(s) are highly visible you are likely to bring more traffic to your site through this resource.

Diversify your internal anchor links is also important. These are the links on your page that the search engines will find when they crawl your site. Finally, make sure your pages have at least 250 words, use fonts that are easy to read and headlines to help divide your page and make it easier to read.

Google will deem good content search worthy and proper use of SEO will help you to place higher in the search engines. Good content with good SEO equals increased traffic to your site.

Decrease Your Bounce Rate Increase Your Free Traffic

If there is one thing search engines hate, it is a high bounce rate. If your bounce rate is too high, Google and other search engines could punish you by decreasing your rank and placement. Decrease your bounce rate and you will be rewarded by the search engines. Better placement means more traffic to your site.

Bounce rate is one of those metrics that is tossed around a lot in the search engines. It's often talked about in absolutes, but it is better to look at bounce rates subjectively.

If you have a high bounce rate it could indicate a number of things that generally will fall into either one of these two categories.

1. You are acquiring the wrong kind of traffic to your site.

2. You are acquiring the right kind of traffic to your site.

Page 16

If you are confused by the second one, you aren't alone. But think about it. If your website provides exactly what the visitor wants or provides a solution to the question the visitor will leave the page quickly. That means you will have a high bounce rate.

You want your visitors to stick around, but you also want them to find what they want. So you need to spread their stay around so that they are checking out more of your site before they leave. This means you want more engaged visitors.

To decrease your bounce rate, you might also

1. Avoid the use of pop ups

2. Use a navigation setup that is intuitive and contains key items

3. Avoid poor website design

4. Increase the rate at which your pages load

5. Make your site mobile friendly

6. Segment your information

7. Optimize for intent

8. Design information based on your priorities

9. Watch where you place ads

10. Remove distractions

11. Leverage internal searches

Decrease your bounce rate and increase your traffic. It's worth your time to work on a better bounce rate.

Page 18

How Accurate Keywords Can Increase Your Free Site Traffic

All of us are always looking for ways to create free traffic for our websites and yet ironically some of the most ethical and easiest ways to increase website traffic are often overlooked. One of those is the use of accurate keywords.

What does that mean? It means that the keywords you choose should accurately reflect the content you have. The reason we use keywords is to help surfers find the content they are looking for. Choosing popular keywords that have nothing to do with your content is a commonly made mistake – don't do it! Instead, find the most popular relevant keyword and use it in your title. Be extremely literal and descriptive in your title and then use your keyword throughout your article several times in a natural way. You should never keyword stuff, because if you do, Google is likely to punish you.

If you have a keyword that's a bit confusing relating to its meaning take your time to explain to them what you are talking about and what the meaning is. When you use your keyword or keyword throughout your article consider using variations of the word(s) and mixing up the order of your keyword phase.

Keywords are powerful. They help you to place better in the search engines, which means when someone searches for your keyword(s) they are more likely to find you, because you show up sooner in the search engines. This translates to more free traffic to your website.

So, now wasn't that easy? Just taking the time to choose the best and most accurate keywords can significantly increase your free traffic flow. It will cost you nothing but a little time and you will enjoy huge benefits for your time. What better time to increase your traffic than right now.

Page 20

Use Social Media to Increase Your Free Traffic

Social media is often overlooked as a method to create an increase in your free traffic. Yet it is significant and can ensure that you have a presence that is solid and that your site is viewed by many.

When you post content that is compelling it won't take long to build a loyal following and that following is going to share with others and they will share with others and so on it goes and soon you'll see a significant increase in your site traffic and it will not have cost you anything. There are a number of ways you can achieve this.

#1 Create a Facebook page to promote your website. This is a great way to share informative posts and send your visitors to your site for more related content. Post regularly and always make sure your posts have value and are not just advertising for your site.

#2 Twitter is a great way to let followers know that you have added new content or articles to your site.
It's also a great way to build new followers who in turn will take the time to visit your site if you have something of interest/value to offer. Make sure you link your Twitter feed to your website and your Facebook feed to your Twitter account.

#3 Tumblr is a social networking site that is often overlooked and yet it is a great tool for bringing free traffic to your site. It is a blogging service that lets you link easily to the content on your site. It is also different in format than most blogging sites in that the sharing of content is done easily and provides a great way to grow your followers.

#4 Pinterest is image based social networking. It began as a place to exchange recipes and crafts, but has grown into a site with numerous categories and it is one of the fastest growing social networking sites on the internet.

#5 Google+ is another social networking site that lets you easily post links to your site and publish content. It has the potential to reach a very large audience, which in turn allows for fast and free growth of traffic to your site.

Page 22

Grow Your Free Traffic by Addressing a Niche Market

If you want to increase your traffic and you want to do it for free, then why not try addressing a niche market. You'll be happy with the results you see!

The best sites address a niche or a specific audience. They become an expert in their field. You want your website to be the resource they first look to for expertise in the field. You want to establish your site as the best resource to go to for your niche.

You can either start a site based on your interests or examine the market and see where a strong niche is that isn't covered very well. You can then take this niche and turn it into an area where you are the expert.

Niche markets are one of the most overlooked tools available to generate free traffic. There are all kinds of websites – millions upon millions and yet still there are many niche markets that either have limited coverage or no coverage at all.

Many who decide to start an online business seek out the most searched terms and build a site around that. The trouble is that's what everyone else is also doing and that means that is where the competition is highest.

Choosing a niche that doesn't have as high of competition means that you are going to have a higher flow of traffic to your site than you would if the competition was stiff. That's one way you will enjoy increased traffic. The other way is simply because surfers are looking for an expert in that niche and once they realize that's what you are they'll not only come to your site they will share your site with others that would also be interested in that niche.

So what are you waiting for? What niche will you choose to increase the traffic to your site?

Page 24

Increase Your Traffic with Great Content

When it comes to increasing organic search, content marketing through blogging or guest posts is the fastest way to build great traffic. However, content marketing is a quality game and not a quantity game. If you have horrible content, people won't bother reading it or sharing it, which is basically the entire point of building a company blog. Therefore, when I write content, I constantly ask myself if I would take ten minutes out of my day to read it and if I'd share it with others. If you wouldn't do either of those things, then you really need to look at your content strategy again.

Search engines are rewarding people and companies who are getting high-quality, consistent content coming from them. Things such as author rank are going to have a big effect on organic search results. Put a plan in place to not only create content to publish online, but also to be able to maximize the value of the content so that it is properly distributed across social channels and has a chance to go viral.

Write articles rich in content. Quality articles will get ranked better in search results. Make sure that your articles address the needs of your readers, and that they can find all of the information they need in one spot. This is the most effective means for increasing traffic to a website; offering people something that they cannot obtain elsewhere, or at least, not to the level of quality that you are offering it.

Whatever you do, don't use content generators. While once a popular choice by a new web industry, today they are not considered useful. It is much better to put creativity to work. Content generated articles will be shunned by Google and other search engines and visitors will be disappointed with the content they find, which means they'll leave your site. Good content will increase your visitors and that will increase your traffic flow.

Never make the mistake of copying and pasting from another site. The search engines are too smart and will know that's what you did. You will be penalized for it and that is going to result in a decrease in traffic.

Page 26

Make Use of Industry Experts to Increase Your Free Traffic

If you want to increase your free traffic to your website become an expert site in your niche. You might be an expert in your niche yourself, which is great, but you can gain even more momentum by using industry experts too.

It won't be that difficult to convince leaders in their industry to contribute guest post on your blog or to do a webinar with you. Experts like to share their knowledge and if it gets them exposure at the same time, they are that much more interested in getting involved.

They will also likely have their own following and those people will now become familiar with your brand or niche. That's another line of free traffic for you that's a bonus!

These experts often produce superior written content that their existing users keep on top of. Your followers are likely to take an interest in it as well and if they are happy with what they read, they'll share it with others and you'll once again see your free traffic grow.

When your followers see that you are brining industry experts onboard as guests they'll be excited to not only participate but also tell others about what's going on within your niche site. That's certainly going to bring additional traffic your way.

Industry experts are respected and often recognized among surfers and visitors alike. Their expertise is a natural draw. People want to see what they have to say. Once they are on your website you will have to figure out how you will keep them there and how you will keep them returning You will also want to put into place a method that will work to invite others so that you continue to see your traffic grow.

Take advantage of Industry experts – they are a powerful tool that is often underutilized.

Page 28

Post to Forums and Blogs to Increase Your Free Website Traffic

So you are looking to increase your free traffic to your website, but find you are struggling with just how to do this. Ironically, and far too often, the most obvious and easiest to use are overlooked. That is the case with forums and blogs – both can be invaluable tools that can provide you with real value in increasing your traffic.

You can visit online discussion forums, and there are many, where people from your target market tend to gather and hang out. Once there you can post responses to questions that are useful and helpful. With that you can include a link to your site with your name at the end of your post. A great way to drive more traffic to your site.

Ultimately, you will want to setup a signature file with a link to your site so that It can be seen as often as possible. This is quicker and more effective than adding it to each post. Do not over post because if you do, you will lose respect and others will choose not to visit your site. You will completely destroy any of the benefits of forum posting.

You can also post to other people's blogs. Leave comments regularly and make sure your website link is always visible when you post. It works the same way as your posts do to forums and here too you want to make sure that you do not over post and annoy others. There are an endless array of blogs available so follow several. It will give you more posting opportunities.

Bottom line – anywhere you can get your information out there and a link to your website take advantage of it and watch your traffic grow – best of all it's free!

Page 30

Proper Tags and Descriptions Can Increase Your Traffic

You want your traffic to grow and you want this to happen for free. So what to do? Great news – an act as simple as ensuring your proper tags and descriptions can increase your traffic flow.

Your tags, metadata and description in your article or content will affect how well they show in Google and the other search engines. It will help you rank better and sit better in the search engines. The more people that see your site in the search engines the more traffic you'll enjoy coming to your site.

If you want to have a completely functional and successful site, you need to ensure that your tags are in place and that you do not have any broken links. You will also need to submit your sitemap to Google so that your website shows in the Google search engine.

Be sure to use your keyword(s) or keyword phrases effectively. This is part of your SEO or search engine optimization strategy and it will aid people in finding your site when they do a search whether in Google or using another search engine. Make sure your keywords are flowing in a manner that is natural with the text. When you are searching for good keywords, make sure you learn what words are most naturally going to come to mind for all ages of visitors and then ensure you include them.

Your primary keyword needs to be in the title, description, meta tags and content. Do not keyword spam because Google and the other search engines will punish you for doing so. Do not bother putting your keyword into your graphic because the search engines cannot pick it up, but you can put it in the alt text that is associated with your image.

Proper tags and descriptions are an easy way to increase your traffic to your site.

Page 32

Increase Your Traffic by Creating Shareable Content

So you want to increase your traffic to your site and you want to do it for free… how do you go about doing that? There are plenty of ways you can do this, but one that we'll look at is to increase your traffic by creating shareable content.

Your content needs to be easily shared so that your visitors can help you spread the word. This is achieved through a combination of using a solid headline and an image that is interesting, along with a solid, captivating lead in.

This combination helps you to create the perfect small chunk of information about your article that can be shared on Twitter, Facebook, Google+ and other social media networks.

Lists are very popular for sharing amongst the many social networks. Sites like Mashable are able to do a fantastic job of using list headlines like "20 Ways to or 10 Signs of." These do a great job of drawing the reader's eye and compensate for short attention spans. You can learn from this site and other similar ones about how to create headings that work.

Your content needs to be interesting if you want anyone to be interested in sharing it with others. So, if you just throw something together expect your visitors to put as much effort into it as you did. It will fail! If you take your time to write something of interest that engages your visitors, they will be very interested in sharing it with other people they know, and those people will share it with others that they know, and so forth, it will grow and grow and grow. Suddenly you have an increase in traffic to your site that's significant and best of off it's free. Now that's how you increase your traffic without spending money.

Page 34

Use Good Web Design to Increase Your Traffic

We become so focused on finding free traffic that we sometimes find ourselves overlooking some of the easiest ways to increase your traffic flow to your website and we can do it for free. One of those key things is your web design. A good web design will increase your traffic. Let's look at some of the important points for your website.

#1 Balance your page – A good website has balance. When a visitor arrives at your page, the first thing they see is the top left of your page. They will hover there before moving up or down the page. Balance will make your page visually appealing and it will make it easier for the visitor to find items when the flow is good.

#2 Build a modern design that is cohesive – If you build a website that is hard to find your way around on, your visitors will hit the back button faster than you can say 'gone.' Make sure that you choose a design and layout that is easy to navigate and easy on the eyes.

#3 Be sure that you keep your page simple. A clean site is much more visually appealing than one that is too busy. We tend to like to use all of the great tools that allow us to put very cool graphics on our site, show videos, interact with visitors, and on it goes. However, we tend to put too many active things on the page and that makes it hard for visitors to stay focused. In fact, it can be annoying. It's not that you shouldn't use these items, but rather choose wisely how you use them.

#4 Create a navigation menu that is easy to use and easy to find all of the content on the site. Web visitors often look for a toolbar across the side or top so make sure that you stay with what visitors will find familiar and don't forget the link back to your home page.

A good web design means visitors stay on your site because they 'like' it and return often. It also means they are far more likely to recommend your site to others. Something as simple as a good web design can increase your free traffic so don't overlook it.

Page 36

Use Long Tail Keywords to Generate Free Traffic

Are you wanting to generate free traffic? Great news – you can do this and you can do it ethically, which ensures you will keep Google and other search engines happy. You can increase the traffic you generate using long tail keywords.

What are long tail keywords? A long tail keyword(s) is specific to that which a searcher looks for. For example, if you sell interior paint, your research might lead you to learn that potential customers might also search 'can you use exterior paint inside."

This is a very specific phase and if you answer this question on your website you can attract traffic related to that term and then from there you can link to your product that would you recommend. You can see how the long tail keyword phrase expands who your visitor might be and that means increased traffic to your site that you might otherwise miss.

To ensure the best value from your keywords, you should implement them on your site in a manner that makes them clear and easy for your visitor to navigate. Take the time to carry out your research properly not only t find your regular keywords but also to find the best long tail keywords. You may find that you need to turn keywords around on some pages or change one word in the keyword phrase. Search is fluid and to enjoy the best results from your keywords you need to also be fluid.

It's helpful to write a number of quality articles on keywords that are very specific. Staying focused with long tail keyword terms also have a better conversion rate. There are a number of tools on the market that can help you determine your best

Page 38

long tail keywords. These tools can help you to focus on the most promising organic keyword(s).

Long tail keywords are often overlooked and that means if you aren't taking advantage of them, you could be missing out on generating an increase in free traffic to your site.

Page 40

Use Traffic Exchanges to Increase Your Free Site Traffic

Are you trying to increase the traffic to your website? Are you looking for free traffic? Then why not take advantage of what a traffic exchange can do for you?

For those of you not familiar with traffic exchanges this is the type of site that offers a service to webmasters in exchange for traffic. It is like the autosurf idea, except with the traffic exchange there is usually a manual rotation. In other words, the traffic exchange will send you traffic in exchange for you sending them traffic

There are various kinds of traffic exchanges but the concept remains the same at all of them. You can search the internet for "traffic exchange" to find a number of these services. Let's look at a scenario where traffic exchange is at work.

Let's say as a web surfer you visit another traffic exchange member's website and you earn credit. You can then use the credit you earned to get other visitors (members) to your website. The traffic that arrives at your site is completely free. There are very few traffic exchange sites that demand members pay for the traffic they send unless you choose to buy a traffic upgrade for your account. You can buy text ads or banner ads.

You can earn money while you surf. Some people have earned $0.2/day with only two traffic exchange sites. Not every traffic exchange site has this kind of feature. You will want to read what is offered by the traffic exchange website before you sign up.

Traffic exchanges are often overlooked as a way to increase free traffic to a website because they are not fully understood. Do not make the same mistake of so many before you. Learn what a traffic exchange is and does, and then put it to work on building traffic for your site.

Page 42

Create a Social Site and Increase Your Free Traffic

Your goal is to increase your free traffic. Great news! If you create a social site you can do exactly that, increase your traffic for no cost. Let's have a s look at what your social site needs to accomplish.

#1 Incorporate Call to Action – Ask your visitors to become involved. If they like what your site has to offer they'll likely return. Your call to action will engage your visitor and ask them to help by inviting others to your site, leaving comments and writing responses.

#2 Make Use of Comments – Comments are a great way for you to interact and engage with your visitors. You can stay in touch and respond to comments that are made. You should allot a few minutes daily to respond to comments that have been made. Engaged visitors come back!

#3 Interact With Other Blogs and Sites – You can stay connected to other blogs and sites that are in your niche. Leave comments on their posts, get involved with these communities and let people find you.

This will increase your traffic. However, don't hog the site and don't be a nuisance. Don't post just for the sake of posting. Make sure you have something of value to add.

#4 Start Your Own Forum – Add a forum to your site. It's a great place for people to gather and discuss everything from A to Z. They can talk about the niche your site handles or about the weather. Active forums are a great way to bring your visibility up in the search engines and that increases your traffic flow. Don't be surprised if your forum grows rapidly – the good ones do. Just be prepared to add a moderator to the site to ensure things remain civil.

These are just four things you can do to create a more social site and increase traffic to your website. Think outside the box and enjoy the growth.

Page 44

Build a Community to Increase Your Free Traffic

You have a website that does okay, but you want to increase the traffic to your site and you want it to be free traffic. Now you are wondering what you can do to achieve your goal? There are many different things you can do. One of them is to build a community.

Increasing your Google traffic is about answering questions that are found to be important in your community. You must take the time to become the authority and have the necessary expertise in your niche.

Have the community ask you questions. By doing so, you will be on your way to providing useful, valuable, high quality content. That's what Google really cares about. When you provide answers to questions asked by your community, Google will rank your website very well for the keyword terms you would not have come up with on your own, but these keywords do show up in your answers to questions.

You create loyalty among your community members and you rank well with Google at the same time. You could say that is a win-win! Now you have members in your community that are going to share and tell others about it, which will increase your traffic flow. That will multiply and continue to grow as more visitors show up and like what you have to offer.

In addition, Google will rank you well so you will place better in the search engines. Doing so means that more surfers will find you and come visit your page for an additional way of increasing the traffic to your site. These people when happy will again invite others.

So when looking for proven ways to increase your traffic flow make sure that you do not overlook the power of community – build a strong niche community and they will come.

Page 46

Give Away Freebies and Increase Your Free Traffic

Freebies can bring your site free traffic. Who doesn't like receiving something free? That's why online freebies are so popular. Freebies bring visitors to your site and when done right they leave the visitor wanting more, which leads to a purchase.

Choosing quality freebies will ensure you have an increase in your free traffic. What do some of the freebies that have value look like? Here are some freebies for you to consider.

#1 E-book – give away an e-book and make sure your ad is on it. Let your visitors also give away the ebook. This will increase your ad exposure and as a result increase your free traffic to your site.

#2 Online Classes – Hold online seminars or classes that are free. You can hold these in a chat room. People love free ways to learn something about what interests them and from there you can send them to your site for more information or to make a purchase. It's an easy way to increase your traffic flow.

#3 Webinars – Webinars are another way to teach people. Offer free webinar classes that also send them to your website. A quick and easy way to increase your traffic flow for no cost.

#4 Contests – Contests are a great way to increase your traffic flow. Give site visitors a free entry and let them enter daily. You will be amazed at how much this can impact your traffic. People love to share contests and that means new free traffic for you.

#5 Software – Give away free software or turn part of your website into an area that contains all kinds of free software available for visitors to download. Make sure your ad is inside. Let others give away this software too. Of course, any software you give away must be legally available to do so.

There are all kinds of things you can give away, depending on your niche market. Don't be afraid to think outside the box. You'll be impressed at the increase you'll enjoy in free traffic.